THE
COUPLES
COMMUNICATION
HANDBOOK

Your Roadmap to Stronger, Healthier Communication and Deeper Connection

INDEX

INTRODUCTION

Welcome to The Couples Communication Handbook, a comprehensive guide designed to help you and your partner navigate the complexities of communication in your relationship.

Whether you're seeking to deepen your connection, resolve conflicts more effectively, or simply improve the way you interact with one another, this handbook offers practical insights and strategies to support you on your journey.

Communication lies at the heart of every healthy relationship. It serves as the cornerstone upon which trust, intimacy, and understanding are built.

Yet, despite its fundamental importance, many couples find themselves grappling with communication challenges that can strain even the strongest bonds.

In this handbook, we'll delve into the various hurdles that couples commonly encounter in their communication, exploring the underlying dynamics that contribute to these issues.

INTRODUCTION

From defensiveness and avoidance to passive-aggressiveness and contempt, each chapter will shine a light on a different aspect of communication breakdowns, offering insights and practical tools to help you overcome them.

But before we dive into specific communication strategies and techniques, it's essential to understand why these challenges arise in the first place. Our upbringing, past experiences, and learned behaviors all shape the way we communicate with our partners.

Childhood traumas, family dynamics, and cultural influences can leave lasting imprints on our communication styles, influencing how we express ourselves and interpret the words and actions of our loved one.

At the core of effective communication lies empathy—the ability to understand and share the feelings of another. Empathy serves as the bridge that connects us to our partners, fostering compassion, validation, and mutual respect.

INTRODUCTION

Throughout this handbook, you'll discover how cultivating empathy can transform the way you communicate, paving the way for deeper connection and intimacy in your relationship.

This handbook is not just about diagnosing communication problems; it's about offering practical solutions and empowering you to enact positive change.

Each chapter will provide valuable insights into common communication pitfalls, along with actionable strategies and exercises to help you navigate them more skillfully.

As you embark on this journey, remember that change doesn't happen overnight. It requires patience, commitment, and a willingness to confront both internal and external obstacles.

But by investing in your relationship and prioritizing open, honest communication, you can cultivate a stronger, more resilient bond with your partner—one built on trust, understanding, and unwavering support.

INTRODUCTION

So, let's embark on this journey together, armed with the tools and insights needed to transform your communication and enrich your relationship.

Whether you're facing longstanding conflicts or simply seeking to enhance your connection, The Couples Communication Handbook is here to guide you every step of the way.

Are you ready to embark on this transformative journey?

Let's dive in.

CHAPTER 1

*"At any given moment you have the power to
say: this is not how my story is going to end."*

– Christine Mason Miller –

CHAPTER 1

In this chapter, we'll explore the fundamental reasons why couples often find themselves struggling with communication in their relationships. From childhood experiences to ingrained patterns of behavior, we'll uncover the underlying dynamics that can hinder effective communication.

Additionally, we'll delve into the pivotal role of empathy—the cornerstone of healthy communication—and how it can serve as a powerful tool for fostering understanding and connection.

WHY DO COUPLES STRUGGLE WITH COMMUNICATION?

Communication is more than just exchanging words; it's about conveying emotions, needs, and desires in a way that fosters understanding and connection.

However, despite its importance, many couples encounter obstacles that impede their ability to communicate effectively.

CHAPTER 1

One significant factor contributing to communication challenges is our upbringing and past experiences. Our early interactions with caregivers, family dynamics, and cultural influences shape the way we communicate with others, particularly in intimate relationships.

Childhood traumas, unresolved conflicts, and learned behaviors can all leave lasting imprints on our communication styles, influencing how we express ourselves and interpret the words and actions of our partners.

Moreover, societal norms and gender roles can also impact communication dynamics within relationships. Traditional expectations around masculinity, femininity, and emotional expression may contribute to misunderstandings and conflicts between partners.

Breaking free from these ingrained stereotypes and embracing authentic communication is essential for fostering healthy, egalitarian relationships.

CHAPTER 1

Throughout history, society has imposed rigid expectations on individuals based on their gender, prescribing specific roles and behaviors deemed appropriate for men and women.

These gender norms often influence how we communicate within relationships, shaping our attitudes towards emotional expression, vulnerability, and power dynamics.

For many years, traditional gender roles have dictated that men should embody traits such as stoicism, dominance, and independence, while women are expected to be nurturing, empathetic, and submissive.

These expectations not only limit individuals' freedom to express themselves authentically but also create barriers to effective communication within relationships.

In heterosexual relationships, these gendered communication patterns can manifest in various ways. Men may feel pressure to suppress their emotions and maintain a facade of strength, fearing that vulnerability will be perceived as weakness.

CHAPTER 1

As a result, they may struggle to express their feelings openly, leading to emotional disconnection and misunderstandings with their partners.

Conversely, women may face expectations to prioritize their partner's needs over their own, suppressing their desires and opinions to maintain harmony in the relationship. This can result in feelings of resentment and dissatisfaction, as their own needs and perspectives are overlooked or invalidated.

Furthermore, traditional gender roles can contribute to unequal power dynamics within relationships, with men often assuming leadership roles and making decisions without consulting their partners.

This imbalance of power can erode trust and mutual respect, undermining the foundation of a healthy, equal partnership.

Breaking free from these ingrained stereotypes requires a concerted effort to challenge and unlearn societal expectations around gender and communication.

CHAPTER 1

It involves recognizing that both men and women are capable of experiencing a full range of emotions and expressing themselves authentically without conforming to narrow gender norms.

Embracing authentic communication means creating space for vulnerability, empathy, and mutual respect within the relationship.

It means valuing each other's perspectives and experiences, regardless of gender, and actively listening to understand rather than to respond.

By challenging traditional gender roles, couples can foster healthier, more fulfilling relationships built on mutual understanding, respect, and partnership.

In the following chapters, we'll explore practical strategies for overcoming communication challenges and cultivating a more authentic connection with your partner.

BENEFITS OF EFFECTIVE COMMUNICATION

- Cultivates Trust: When you and your partner communicate openly and honestly, it creates a safe space for trust to flourish. Trust is the cornerstone of any successful relationship.

- Resolves Conflicts: Conflict is inevitable in any relationship, but how you handle it can make all the difference. Effective communication provides the tools and strategies to navigate conflicts in a constructive and respectful manner. It allows you and your partner to address issues, find common ground, and work towards resolutions together.

- Enhances Understanding and Empathy: Communication is not just about expressing your own thoughts and feelings; it's also about actively listening and understanding your partner's perspective. When you truly listen and empathize with your partner, it deepens your understanding of each other.

CHAPTER 1

- Strengthens Emotional Bond: **By communicating openly and honestly, you create a space for vulnerability and emotional intimacy. Sharing your thoughts, fears, dreams, and desires with your partner strengthens the emotional bond between you, creating a deeper sense of closeness and connection.**

- Establishes Healthy Boundaries: **Effective communication allows you and your partner to establish and respect each other's boundaries. It enables you to express your needs and desires while also understanding and honoring your partner's boundaries. This mutual understanding promotes a healthier and more balanced relationship.**

- Creates a Supportive and Validating Space: **When you communicate effectively, you create a supportive and validating space for both you and your partner. It allows you to celebrate each other's successes, provide comfort during difficult times, and offer encouragement and validation in your everyday lives.**

CHAPTER 1

THE ROLE OF EMPATHY IN COMMUNICATION

Empathy—the ability to understand and share the feelings of another—is the bedrock of effective communication. It enables us to see the world through our partner's eyes, validating their emotions and experiences even when we may not fully understand them ourselves.

By cultivating empathy, we can bridge the gap between differing perspectives, fostering mutual respect and compassion in our relationships.

Empathy involves more than just listening; it requires active engagement and genuine curiosity about our partner's inner world.

It means setting aside our own judgments and assumptions to truly connect with their thoughts and feelings.

When we approach communication with empathy, we create a safe space for vulnerability and authenticity, laying the foundation for deeper emotional intimacy and trust.

CHAPTER 1

THE ROLE OF EMPATHY IN COMMUNICATION

In the following chapters, we'll explore specific communication challenges that couples commonly encounter, from defensiveness and avoidance to criticism and contempt.

Each chapter will offer insights into the underlying triggers and dynamics of these behaviors, along with practical strategies and exercises to help you overcome them.

By understanding the root causes of communication challenges and embracing empathy as our guiding principle, we can cultivate healthier, more fulfilling relationships with our partners.

Are you ready to embark on this journey of self-discovery and growth? Let's dive into Chapter 2 and explore how defensiveness can impact communication in relationships.

NOTES

NOTES

NOTES

NOTES

CHAPTER 2

"Defensiveness is the armor we put on to protect ourselves, but it's also the barrier that keeps us from truly connecting with others. Break down the walls of defensiveness and watch your relationships flourish."

– Brené Brown –

CHAPTER 2

In this chapter, we'll delve into one of the most common barriers to effective communication in relationships: defensiveness.

Whether in response to criticism, conflict, or perceived threats to our self-image, defensiveness can hinder our ability to engage in open, honest dialogue with our partners.

We'll explore the underlying triggers and dynamics of defensiveness, along with practical strategies and exercises to help you overcome this barrier and foster healthier communication patterns in your relationship.

UNDERSTANDING DEFENSIVENESS

Defensiveness is a natural response to feeling attacked, criticized, or misunderstood.

When we perceive a threat to our sense of self-worth or integrity, our instinctual reaction is to protect ourselves, often by deflecting blame, making excuses, or counter-attacking.

CHAPTER 2

While this defense mechanism may offer temporary relief from discomfort, it ultimately exacerbates conflict and undermines the trust and connection between partners.

COMMON TRIGGERS OF DEFENSIVENESS

Defensiveness can be triggered by a variety of factors, ranging from external criticism to internal insecurities.

Understanding these triggers can help individuals recognize and address their defensive reactions more effectively. Here are some common triggers of defensiveness in relationships:

- Perceived Criticism: Criticism, whether real or perceived, is a primary trigger of defensiveness in relationships. When we feel attacked or judged by our partner's words or actions, our instinctual response is often to protect ourselves by becoming defensive. Even well-intentioned feedback can be interpreted as criticism if it challenges our sense of self-worth or competence.

- Fear of Rejection: **Past experiences of rejection or abandonment can leave lasting emotional scars that make us hypersensitive to perceived threats to our relationships. When we fear being rejected or abandoned by our partner, we may react defensively to any sign of disapproval or disagreement, fearing that it may signal the end of the relationship.**

- Insecurities and Self-Doubt: **Low self-esteem and feelings of inadequacy can heighten our sensitivity to criticism and rejection, making us more prone to defensive reactions. When we don't feel confident in ourselves or our abilities, even minor setbacks or criticisms can feel like personal attacks on our worthiness as individuals.**

- Threats to Self-Image: **Defensiveness often arises when our sense of self-image or identity is threatened. For example, if we pride ourselves on being a good partner or parent, any suggestion that we've fallen short in these roles can trigger defensive reactions.**

- Unresolved Emotions: Unresolved emotions from past conflicts or traumas can fuel defensive reactions in present interactions. When we haven't fully processed or addressed our feelings about a particular issue, we may become defensive when it's brought up again, fearing that it will reopen old wounds or lead to further conflict.

- Lack of Trust: Trust issues in the relationship can also contribute to defensiveness, as individuals may perceive their partner's words or actions with skepticism or suspicion. When trust is compromised, even innocent remarks or questions may be interpreted as veiled criticisms or accusations, triggering defensive responses.

- Feeling Powerless or Threatened: Defensiveness can also arise from feelings of powerlessness or threat in the relationship. If one partner feels marginalized or disregarded in decision-making processes, they may resort to defensiveness as a way of asserting their autonomy and protecting their interests.

CHAPTER 2

- Cultural and Gender Expectations: Societal norms and gender roles can also play a role in triggering defensiveness in relationships. For example, men may feel pressure to maintain a facade of strength and competence, while women may feel compelled to prioritize their partner's needs over their own. When these expectations are challenged, individuals may respond defensively to protect their gender identity and social status.

THE HIDDEN PAIN BEHIND DEFENSIVENESS

"I was never made to feel good enough"

"I was often shamed, criticized, or bullied"

"I didn't feel safe growing up"

"I had to keep my guard up to protect myself"

"I didn't feel like people cared about me"

"I was made to feel inadequate & unlovable"

CHAPTER 2

EXAMPLES OF DEFENSIVENESS

Defensive behavior can manifest in various ways, often as a response to feeling threatened, criticized, or vulnerable. Here are some common examples of how defensive behavior might look in a romantic relationship:

- Denial or Minimization: The individual may deny responsibility for their actions or downplay the significance of their partner's concerns. They might say things like, "I didn't do anything wrong" or "It's not that big of a deal."

- Blame-Shifting: Instead of taking accountability, the defensive person may shift blame onto their partner or external factors. They might say things like, "You're overreacting" or "If you hadn't done/said [X], this wouldn't have happened."

- Counterattacks: When feeling attacked or criticized, the defensive individual may respond with their own accusations or criticisms. They might deflect attention away from the issue at hand by bringing up past grievances or unrelated topics.

- Justification: They may offer explanations or excuses for their behavior rather than acknowledging the impact it had on their partner. This could involve rationalizing their actions or providing context that undermines their partner's feelings.

- Withdrawal or Stonewalling: Some individuals may shut down emotionally or physically withdraw from the conversation as a defense mechanism. They might become silent, leave the room, or refuse to engage further in the discussion.

- Avoidance: Rather than addressing the issue directly, the defensive person may change the subject or avoid discussing it altogether. They might distract their partner with unrelated topics or make plans to leave the situation.

- Defensiveness Through Humor: Using humor as a defense mechanism, they might make light of the situation or joke about their partner's concerns in an attempt to deflect attention away from the underlying issues.

- Dismissiveness: They may invalidate their partner's feelings or perspectives, dismissing them as irrational or unwarranted. This can leave the partner feeling unheard or unimportant in the relationship.

- Overexplaining: In an effort to justify their actions, the defensive individual may provide excessive explanations or details, hoping to convince their partner of their innocence or good intentions.

SIGNS OF DEFENSIVENESS IN YOURSELF OR YOUR PARTNER

As mentioned before, defensiveness can manifest in various ways, some more subtle than others.

Recognizing these signs is the first step toward addressing and mitigating their impact on your relationship. This is defensive behavior:

- Withdrawing into silence
- Tell your partner not to feel the way they feel

- Justifying the behavior or words instead of apologizing
- Choosing not to listen to your partner's perspective
- Getting angry and verbally attacking
- Putting the blame back on your partner
- Not willing to compromise or resolve
- Playing the victim
- Making excuses about the concerns that are brought up
- Minimizing the partner's feelings or concerns
- Interrupting or talking over the partner
- Reacting with sarcasm or contempt
- Avoiding responsibility by shifting focus to unrelated issues

THE IMPACT OF DEFENSIVENESS ON COMMUNICATION

Defensiveness is like a wall that we erect between ourselves and our partners, preventing authentic connection and understanding.

When we become defensive, we're more focused on protecting our ego than on truly listening to and empathizing with our partner's perspective.

This can lead to a breakdown in communication, with both partners feeling unheard, invalidated, and frustrated. Moreover, defensiveness tends to escalate conflict rather than resolve it.

When one partner becomes defensive, the other may respond with further criticism or aggression, creating a destructive cycle of blame and resentment.

Over time, this pattern erodes trust and intimacy, making it increasingly difficult to address issues and resolve conflicts in a constructive manner.

WHAT ABOUT THE PERSON ON THE RECEIVING END?

Ever felt like you're tiptoeing through a field of eggshells, trying not to set off any alarms? That's a day in the life when you're on the receiving end of defensiveness. It's like every word you say has to pass through a "Will this cause a blow-up?" filter. And let's be real, it's exhausting. You start to dodge conversations and swallow words to keep the peace.

CHAPTER 2

Imagine this: You want to talk about something that's been bugging you, but the memory of past arguments holds you back. You're mentally rehearsing your words, aiming for "gentle" and "non-accusatory," but still, there's a pit in your stomach. It's not just about avoiding conflict; it's about preserving peace, even if it means sacrificing your own peace of mind.

This is tiring, and it often leads to unresolved issues piling up, turning into a giant snowball of discomfort and tension. The cost of constantly avoiding those defensive triggers? Your voice gets lost in the process.

Important things go unsaid, and over time, this silence takes a toll on the relationship's intimacy and trust. It's like there's an invisible barrier between you and your partner, one that keeps the real, meaningful conversations at bay.

COMMUNICATE YOUR NEEDS WITHOUT ATTACKING

So, how do you break this cycle? How do you communicate in a way that doesn't send your partner into defense mode? It's all about approach, timing, and wording.

CHAPTER 2

- Pick Your Moment: Timing is everything. Bringing up a sensitive topic right when your partner walks in from a stressful day is like lighting a match next to a powder keg. Wait for a calm moment, maybe over a casual coffee on a lazy Sunday morning.

- It's Not What You Say, But How You Say It: Start with "I feel" statements rather than "You always." It's about expressing how something affects you, not accusing them of doing something wrong. "I feel overlooked when decisions are made without my input" lands way softer than "You never ask me what I think!"

- Be a Team: Remind your partner that you're not on opposite sides. Use "we" to signal that you're in this together. "How can we work on making decisions together?" feels a lot more inclusive.

- Never say 'never' or 'always': Using extreme language like 'you never' or 'you always' can escalate tensions and make your partner feel defensive. Instead, focus on specific behaviors or situations and how they impact you.

CHAPTER 2

PHRASES TO USE WHEN YOU NOTICE YOUR PARTNER BECOMING DEFENSIVE

"Hey, I just want to remind you that I'm on your side. Can we pause for a moment to reconnect right now?"

"Can we talk about what happened earlier today? I don't want to blame each other. I just want to hear what occurred and share how we felt."

"I'm trying to understand your point of view, but this context is confusing for me. Can we take a break to clear our heads first? Then, we can come up with a strategy for us to talk."

"Did I say something to make you believe I was criticizing you? If so, that's not my intention at all and I'm happy to rephrase my ask."

"I want to talk to you about _____. When I've brought this issue up in the past, I noticed you felt attacked. What can I do to make this conversation better?"

CHAPTER 2

"I value our connection, and I want us to communicate openly without any defenses. Can we take a moment to reset and come back to this?"

"It seems like this topic is hitting a nerve for both of us. Let's take a breather and revisit it when we're both feeling calmer."

WHAT NOT TO SAY

"You're overreacting."

"You always get defensive whenever we talk about this."

"Stop being so sensitive."

"Why are you making such a big deal out of this?"

"You're just being irrational."

"You're being dramatic."

"I can't believe you're getting upset about this."

"You're being too emotional."

"You're just being paranoid."

"This shouldn't bother you."

"You're blowing things out of proportion."

"Why can't you just let it go?"

CHAPTER 2

"You're taking this the wrong way."

"Why are you making this about you?"

"You're not listening to me."

"I can't talk to you when you're like this."

"You're just looking for a fight."

"You're being unreasonable."

"Why are you always so defensive?"

"Stop playing the victim."

"You're making this harder than it needs to be."

"You're impossible to talk to."

STRATEGIES FOR OVERCOMING DEFENSIVENESS

Overcoming defensiveness requires a willingness to cultivate self-awareness, empathy, and vulnerability in our interactions with our partners.

Here are some strategies to help you break free from defensive patterns and foster more open, honest communication:

CHAPTER 2

- **Pause and Reflect:** When you feel yourself becoming defensive, take a moment to pause and reflect on your emotional reaction. Ask yourself why you're feeling defensive and what underlying fears or insecurities may be driving your response.

- **Practice Active Listening:** Instead of immediately jumping to your own defense, make a conscious effort to listen to your partner's perspective with an open mind and heart. Seek to understand their feelings and concerns without judgment or defensiveness.

- **Validate Your Partner's Feelings:** Acknowledge your partner's emotions and experiences, even if you don't agree with their perspective. Let them know that you hear and respect their point of view, fostering a sense of validation and empathy in the conversation.

- **Take Ownership of Your Part:** Instead of deflecting blame or making excuses, take responsibility for your actions and their impact on your partner. Apologize if necessary and commit to finding a constructive solution to the issue at hand.

CHAPTER 2

- Seek Common Ground: Look for areas of agreement or shared values that can serve as a foundation for resolving conflict and rebuilding trust. Focus on finding mutually beneficial solutions rather than "winning" the argument.

Always be honest with your partner about how you are feeling. You could say something like this:

"Hey, I'm feeling myself getting defensive right now, and I want to talk about it. I realize that my reaction might not be helpful, and I want to understand where you're coming from. Can we take a moment to pause and reset so we can have a more constructive conversation?"

Now that we've explored strategies for overcoming defensiveness, it's time to put them into practice.

The following worksheets are designed to help you apply these strategies in real-life situations and deepen your understanding of your communication patterns with your partner.

WORKSHEET

REFLECTIVE QUESTIONS

- **Identify Triggers:** Take some time to reflect on recent interactions with your partner where you felt defensive. What specific words, actions, or situations triggered your defensive reaction? Were there any patterns or recurring themes in these interactions?

- **Explore Underlying Emotions:** Dig deeper into the emotions that arise when you feel defensive. What feelings or fears are driving your defensive reactions? Are you feeling criticized, rejected, or misunderstood? How do these emotions relate to past experiences or insecurities?

- **Examine Self-Talk:** Pay attention to the internal dialogue that accompanies your defensive reactions. What thoughts or beliefs do you tell yourself when you feel defensive? Are there any underlying assumptions or distortions in your thinking that contribute to your defensiveness?

WORKSHEET

- Consider Alternative Perspectives: Challenge yourself to see the situation from your partner's perspective. What might they be feeling or experiencing in this moment? How might their intentions differ from your interpretation of their words or actions? How does considering their perspective change your understanding of the situation?

- Evaluate the Impact: Reflect on the consequences of your defensive reactions on your relationship. How does defensiveness affect the quality of communication and connection with your partner? What opportunities for growth and resolution might be missed when you react defensively?

- Identify Healthy Responses: Brainstorm alternative ways of responding to triggers of defensiveness. How could you express your thoughts and feelings assertively without becoming defensive? What strategies or coping mechanisms could help you regulate your emotions and respond more calmly in challenging situations?

WORKSHEET

- Practice Self-Compassion: Be gentle with yourself as you navigate your defensive tendencies. Recognize that defensiveness is a natural response to feeling threatened or vulnerable. Offer yourself compassion and understanding as you work towards overcoming defensiveness and fostering healthier communication habits.

By engaging in these reflective exercises, you can gain deeper insight into the root causes of your defensiveness and develop strategies for responding more constructively in challenging situations.

Remember that overcoming defensiveness is a gradual process that requires patience, self-awareness, and a commitment to growth.

As you continue to practice non-defensive communication, you'll cultivate greater empathy, understanding, and connection in your relationship.

In this chapter, we've explored the pervasive influence of defensiveness on communication in relationships.

WORKSHEET

We've identified common triggers of defensiveness, ranging from perceived criticism to unresolved emotions, and delved into the underlying dynamics that fuel defensive reactions.

Through reflective questioning, we've encouraged you to uncover the root causes of their defensiveness and consider alternative perspectives on challenging situations.

Understanding defensiveness is the first step towards overcoming it. By cultivating self-awareness and exploring the emotions and beliefs that underlie our defensive reactions, we can begin to dismantle the barriers that hinder open, honest communication with our partners.

Through practicing empathy, active listening, and self-compassion, we can learn to respond to triggers of defensiveness with curiosity and vulnerability rather than deflection and aggression.

As you continue on your journey towards non-defensive communication, remember that change takes time and effort.

WORKSHEET

Be patient with yourself and with your partner as you navigate the complexities of communication in your relationship.

Embrace each opportunity for growth and learning, and celebrate the progress you make along the way.

In the next chapter, we'll delve into another common communication challenge: navigating difficult conversations.

We'll explore strategies for initiating and engaging in conversations about sensitive topics, fostering mutual understanding and respect in the process.

Through practical exercises and insights, we'll empower you to approach difficult conversations with confidence and compassion, laying the groundwork for deeper connection and intimacy in your relationship.

Are you ready to continue your journey towards healthier communication with your partner? Let's dive into Chapter 3 and explore how to navigate difficult conversations with grace and authenticity.

NOTES

NOTES

NOTES

NOTES

NOTES

CHAPTER 3

"Avoidance is the best short-term strategy to escape conflict, and the best long-term strategy to ensure suffering."

- Brendon Burchard -

CHAPTER 3

We've all been there. A crucial conversation looms, and suddenly cleaning the oven, catching up on work emails, or scrolling mindlessly through social media seems infinitely more appealing than actually facing the issue at hand.

This is avoidance, a common communication hurdle that plagues many relationships. While the urge to evade discomfort is understandable, it ultimately hinders our ability to build strong, healthy connections.

In this chapter, we'll delve deeper into the complexities of avoidance in communication, exploring its triggers, consequences, and, most importantly, strategies to overcome it.

UNDERSTANDING AVOIDANCE IN COMMUNICATION

Avoidance refers to a communication pattern where we actively or passively evade difficult topics, emotions, or situations. At its core, avoiding difficult conversations is about fear. Fear of conflict, certainly, but also fear of exposing our vulnerabilities, fear of not being heard, and fear of hurting or being hurt.

CHAPTER 3

While avoidance might seem like a temporary solution to discomfort, it ultimately prevents us from addressing underlying issues and fostering genuine connection with our partners.

COMMON TRIGGERS OF AVOIDANCE

Several factors can trigger avoidance behavior in relationships. Understanding these triggers can help individuals recognize and address this behavior more effectively. Here are some common culprits:

- Fear of conflict: The apprehension of arguments, disagreements, or emotional turmoil can lead individuals to avoid situations that might trigger them. This fear can stem from past negative experiences with conflict or a general dislike of confrontation.

- Discomfort with vulnerability: Sharing genuine emotions and insecurities can feel risky, prompting individuals to withdraw to avoid potential judgment, hurt, or rejection. This can be particularly challenging for individuals who haven't learned healthy ways to express vulnerability in their relationships.

- Uncertainty about how to address issues: Lacking the communication skills or knowledge to navigate challenging conversations effectively can lead to avoidance. This can be especially true for individuals who haven't been exposed to healthy communication models or haven't developed the necessary skills to express themselves clearly and assertively.

- Past experiences of negative communication: Individuals who have experienced negative communication patterns in past relationships, such as constant criticism, blame, or emotional manipulation, might be more prone to avoidance as a way to protect themselves from similar experiences.

THE HIDDEN PAIN BEHIND AVOIDANCE IN COMMUNICATION

While avoidance might appear on the surface as a self-protective mechanism, it often stems from deeper emotions and beliefs.

Here are some of the hidden pains that can fuel avoidance:

- Fear of rejection: The fear of being disliked, abandoned, or judged if we bring up difficult topics can lead us to avoid them altogether, even at the expense of our own needs or the relationship's health.

- Desire to maintain harmony: A strong, and sometimes unrealistic, need to preserve peace and avoid any potential conflict or tension in the relationship. This can stem from a belief that any negativity is detrimental to the relationship, even though healthy conflict can be an opportunity for growth and understanding.

- Unresolved childhood experiences: Individuals who have experienced neglect, invalidation, or emotional abuse in childhood might be hesitant to express themselves openly or engage in vulnerable conversations, fearing repetition of past hurts.

EXAMPLES OF AVOIDANCE IN COMMUNICATION:

Let's see how avoidance can play out in everyday scenarios:

- Imagine John and Sarah are discussing finances. John, uncomfortable with the conversation and afraid of potential arguments about spending habits, starts making jokes, deflecting from addressing the actual issue. This not only avoids the conversation but can also send mixed messages to Sarah, leaving her feeling confused and unheard.

- During a disagreement, Emily shuts down emotionally, refusing to speak or engage with her partner, leaving him feeling unheard, frustrated, and unsure how to proceed. This behavior, while seemingly protecting Emily from further emotional distress, prevents them from finding a solution together.

- David avoids mentioning his concerns about his partner's work schedule, fearing it might lead to an argument or create tension. This bottled-up frustration not only affects his own well-being but can also lead to resentment and distance in the relationship.

CHAPTER 3

THE SIGNS OF AVOIDANCE IN COMMUNICATION

- Changing the subject abruptly when a sensitive topic arises.
- Using humor or sarcasm to deflect serious conversations.
- Engaging in activities or tasks to avoid having to talk about important matters.
- Ignoring messages or calls from the other person when the conversation becomes uncomfortable.
- Making excuses to leave or avoid being in situations where discussions might occur.
- Using vague or non-committal responses to avoid giving a clear opinion or stance.
- Showing physical signs of discomfort, such as fidgeting or avoiding eye contact, during difficult conversations.
- Frequently postponing or delaying discussions about important issues.
- Resorting to passive-aggressive behavior rather than addressing concerns directly.
- Shutting down emotionally or becoming distant when faced with challenging topics.

CHAPTER 3

THE IMPACT OF AVOIDANCE ON YOUR RELATIONSHIP

The consequences of avoidance can be far-reaching, hindering communication and impacting the relationship negatively:

- Unresolved conflicts: When issues are continuously avoided, they remain unaddressed, potentially festering and escalating later. This can lead to bigger blowouts down the line.

- Resentment: Unexpressed feelings and unaddressed issues can build up, leading to resentment and a sense of distance between partners. Over time, this resentment can erode trust and make it difficult for couples to feel close and connected.

Missed opportunities for growth: Avoiding difficult conversations hinders personal growth and the ability to resolve issues constructively as a couple. By facing challenges head-on and practicing healthy communication, partners learn to navigate conflict effectively, strengthen their bond, and grow together.

- Lack of intimacy and connection: Avoidance prevents couples from building trust and fostering deeper emotional connection.

WHAT ABOUT THE PERSON ON THE RECEIVING END?

While the focus has been on the person who avoids communication, it's crucial to consider the impact of avoidance on the partner who is not initiating it. They may experience:

- Frustration: Feeling unheard, misunderstood, and unable to address important issues can lead to significant frustration and a sense of being stuck in a cycle of unresolved issues. This can lead to feelings of helplessness and resentment towards the partner who avoids communication.

- Rejection: Avoidance can be perceived as a form of emotional rejection, leading to feelings of hurt, disconnection, and isolation.

When a partner consistently avoids addressing concerns or sharing their feelings, it can leave the other partner feeling unloved, unimportant, and questioning the foundation of the relationship.

- Lack of trust: When difficult topics are continuously avoided, it can erode trust and create doubt in the relationship's strength and commitment. This can create a sense of insecurity and make it difficult for the partner on the receiving end to feel safe and secure in the relationship.

It's important to remember that avoidance is rarely a deliberate attempt to hurt the other person. However, it's crucial to acknowledge the negative impact it can have and seek ways to address it as a couple.

HOW TO START HAVING DIFFICULT CONVERSATIONS

For couples who typically avoid hard conversations, addressing this pattern requires intentional effort, patience, and often, a change in perspective on how they view and handle conflict.

CHAPTER 3

The heart of any successful conversation lies in how you communicate. It's about expressing your thoughts and feelings clearly and listening to understand, not just to respond.

ACKNOWLEDGE THE ISSUE

- Mutual Recognition: **Both partners need to recognize and acknowledge that avoiding difficult conversations is harming their relationship.**

- Openness to Change: **Commit to addressing the issue together, understanding that it will take time and effort from both sides.**

START SMALL

- Choose Less Challenging Topics: **Begin with topics that are somewhat easier to discuss and gradually work your way up to more sensitive subjects.**

- Positive Reinforcement: **Acknowledge and appreciate each other's efforts to engage in these conversations, reinforcing positive experiences.**

CHAPTER 3

CREATE A SAFE SPACE

- Set Ground Rules: **Agree on rules that make both partners feel safe during discussions, such as no interrupting, yelling, or using hurtful language.**

- Choose the Right Time and Place: **Ensure you're both in the right frame of mind and in a private, comfortable setting without distractions**

PRACTICE PATIENCE & COMPASSION

- Be Patient: **Changing long-standing patterns takes time. Be patient with yourselves and each other.**

- Show Compassion: **Recognize that both of you are doing your best to navigate these challenges.**

PRACTICE MAKES PERFECT

- One way to start having deeper conversations, which will set the stage for future difficult conversations, is to ask each other questions.

CHAPTER 3

Now, you can find many books and cards online but I'll give you 20 questions that will start the conversation right away:

- What experience from your past do you think has shaped your fear of conflict or difficult conversations?

- How do you feel loved and supported during times of conflict or stress?

- What are your deepest insecurities, and how can I help you feel more secure?

- Can you share a time when you felt misunderstood by me? How can we prevent that in the future?

- What is something you've never told me because you were afraid of how I'd react?

- How do our different communication styles affect our relationship, and how can we improve them to support each other better?

- What do you need from me that you feel you're not currently getting?

CHAPTER 3

- How can we make our relationship a safe space where both of us feel comfortable sharing our true thoughts and feelings?

- What dreams or goals have you put aside, and how can I support you in pursuing them?

- What does a truly fulfilling life look like to you, and how does our relationship fit into that vision?

- Is there a part of your identity or past you feel I don't understand fully? How can we bridge that gap?

- How do you deal with anger or frustration in our relationship, and what can we do to handle it more constructively?

- What are your biggest fears about our future together, and how can we address them together?

- What aspect of our relationship do you think needs the most improvement, and how can we work on it together?

CHAPTER 3

- How do you feel about our intimacy? Is there anything you wish was different?

- What have you learned from our relationship that has changed you as a person?

- How can we better communicate our needs and desires to each other without fear of judgment or rejection?

- What actions or words do I use that make you feel unloved or undervalued, possibly without my realization?

- In what ways do you think we've grown together, and what challenges do you see us facing in the future?

- How can we maintain our individuality while growing as a couple?

PROMPTS THAT CAN HELP YOU START DIFFICULT CONVERSATIONS

Initiating difficult conversations requires courage and tact, especially in a relationship where emotions run high, and stakes are significant. Using the right phrases and prompts can help set a constructive tone and open the door to meaningful dialogue.

Here are some phrases and prompts that can help start difficult conversations in a respectful and open-hearted manner:

OPENING PHRASES TO SET A POSITIVE TONE

- "I value our relationship and want us to be honest with each other, even when it's hard. Can we talk about something that's been on my mind?"

- "I've been feeling [emotion] about [topic], and I think it's important we talk about it. When is a good time for you?"

- "There's something I've been struggling with, and I need your help to work through it. Can we discuss it together?"

PROMPTS TO ENCOURAGE OPEN COMMUNICATION

- "Can you share your thoughts on [topic]? I really want to understand your perspective."

- "I noticed that we've been avoiding talking about [topic], and I think it might be affecting us. Can we explore this together?"

- "I feel like we've been distant lately, especially around [topic]. I miss being close to you. Can we talk about what's been going on?"

PHRASES TO FOSTER A SAFE ENVIRONMENT

- "It's important to me that we both feel safe and heard in this conversation. Let's make sure to listen to each other fully before responding."

- "I want to talk about [topic], but I'm not exactly sure how to say it perfectly. Can you bear with me as I try to express what's on my mind?"

- "I've noticed [specific behavior], and it made me feel [emotion]. I don't want to assume anything, so I'd like to hear your thoughts on this."

NAVIGATING DIFFICULT MOMENTS

Even with the best intentions, tough conversations can hit snags. Here's how to keep things on track:

- Stay on Topic: Avoid bringing up past issues not directly related to the conversation at hand. Focus on one topic at a time.

- Seek to Understand: Ask open-ended questions to explore your partner's perspective. Showing genuine curiosity can open doors to compromise and solutions.

CHAPTER 3

MORE PHRASES YOU CAN SAY TO START DIFFICULT CONVERSATIONS

"Hey, I've got something on my mind that I've been wanting to chat with you about."

"Can we have a real talk for a sec? There's something bugging me, and I think we should have a conversation about it."

"Hey, can we talk about something a bit tricky? I've got some thoughts I need to share."

"So, there's this thing I've been avoiding mentioning, but I think we need to talk about it so we can find a solution."

"Something's been bothering me and I need to share. Can we have a heart-to-heart?"

"Listen, I've been feeling a bit uneasy about something and I think we need to chat about it."

"Babe, can we have a serious moment? There's been something bothering me and I need to talk about it."

CHAPTER 3

"Hey, I've been doing some thinking lately, and there's something I really want to discuss with you."

"There's a topic that's been on my mind and I'd love your perspective. Can we have a chat?"

WHAT NOT TO SAY AND WHY:

"Okay, before you jump down my throat, hear me out on this."

"I know you might not want to hear this, but please hear me out before you react."

"I need to talk about something, but promise me you won't be angry."

These phrases, while expressing a desire to communicate openly, may inadvertently set a defensive tone or imply an expectation of negative reactions from the partner.

WORKSHEET

REFLECTIVE QUESTIONS

- **Identify Triggers:** Identifying Triggers: What situations, emotions, or topics typically trigger avoidance behavior in you? (e.g., disagreements, discussing finances, expressing vulnerabilities)

- **Unveiling Fears:** What fears or anxieties arise when you face these triggers? (e.g., fear of conflict, fear of rejection, fear of judgment)

- **Examining Consequences:** How does avoidance behavior impact you and your relationship? (e.g., feelings of guilt, unresolved conflicts, communication breakdown)

- **Developing Coping Mechanisms:** What healthy coping mechanisms can you use to manage discomfort during difficult conversations? (e.g., deep breathing, journaling, relaxation exercises)

Remember, communication is a continuous learning process.

WORKSHEET

REFLECTIVE QUESTIONS

This worksheet is just a starting point to help you navigate challenging conversations with courage and compassion.

By actively engaging in self-reflection and practicing healthy communication skills, you can build stronger, more resilient relationships.

NOTES

NOTES

NOTES

NOTES

CHAPTER 4

*"The worst distance between two people is misunderstanding, and
the most deadly silence is the one that follows an argument."*

– Paulo Coelho –

CHAPTER 4

Communication is the lifeblood of any healthy relationship. However, sometimes silence becomes a weapon, manifesting in the form of silent treatment and stonewalling. These emotionally manipulative tactics can leave the receiver feeling hurt, confused, and disconnected. In this chapter, we'll delve into the complexities of silent treatment and stonewalling, exploring their underlying motivations, the impact they have on relationships, and most importantly, strategies to overcome them and re-establish healthy communication.

UNDERSTANDING SILENT TREATMENT AND STONEWALLING

While both involve withdrawing from communication, there are subtle differences between silent treatment and stonewalling:

Silent treatment:

This involves intentionally withholding communication as a form of punishment or manipulation. It manifests through refusing to talk, responding to texts or calls, or maintaining a cold and distant demeanor. It's like slamming a metaphorical door, leaving the partner feeling shut out and ostracized.

Stonewalling:

This is a broader term encompassing a spectrum of withdrawal behaviors. It can include emotional withdrawal (shutting down emotionally), giving non-verbal cues of disengagement (avoiding eye contact, crossing arms), or resorting to silence as a way of deflecting conflict.

Stonewalling can be like building a wall of emotional unavailability, preventing genuine connection and understanding.

COMMON TRIGGERS OF SILENT TREATMENT AND STONEWALLING

CHAPTER 4

Several factors can trigger these harmful communication tactics:

- Fear of conflict: Individuals with a strong aversion to conflict might retreat into silence to avoid arguments or disagreements, hoping the issue will simply disappear.

- Inability to express emotions healthily: Individuals who struggle with expressing their emotions constructively might withdraw as a way of coping with difficult situations, unsure how to navigate them effectively.

- Desire for control: The silent treatment can be used as a power play to control the other person and manipulate the situation to their advantage, attempting to gain the upper hand through emotional manipulation.

- Past experiences: Individuals who have experienced negative communication patterns in past relationships, marked by constant arguments or emotional abuse, might resort to silence as a self-protective mechanism, fearing similar experiences.

CHAPTER 4

THE HIDDEN PAIN BEHIND SILENT TREATMENT AND STONEWALLING

While these behaviors may appear to be a way of avoiding conflict, they often stem from deeper emotional struggles:

- Fear of intimacy: The fear of getting close and vulnerable can lead individuals to withdraw and push their partner away through silence, afraid of the emotional risks involved in true intimacy.

- Unresolved childhood experiences: Individuals who experienced emotional neglect or invalidation in childhood might struggle with healthy emotional expression and resort to withdrawal as a coping mechanism, having never learned healthy ways to communicate their needs and feelings.

- Low self-esteem: Individuals with low self-esteem might struggle to assert themselves effectively and resort to silence as a way of avoiding potential judgment or rejection, fearing they won't be heard or understood if they speak up.

CHAPTER 4

SIGNS OF SILENT TREATMENT AND STONEWALLING

Being aware of the signs can help you identify these harmful behaviors in your relationship:

Verbal:

- Refusal to talk, respond to questions, or engage in conversation. This can range from complete silence to curt responses that shut down further communication.

- Giving one-word answers or dismissive statements. These minimal responses convey a lack of interest in engaging in a meaningful conversation.

Non-verbal:

- Avoiding eye contact. This can indicate discomfort, a lack of engagement, or a desire to disengage from the situation.

- Withdrawal of physical affection. This can be a way of creating emotional distance and pushing the partner away.

- Crossed arms, closed posture, and lack of facial expressions: These nonverbal cues convey a sense of withdrawal, disengagement, and a lack of openness to communication.

- Changing the subject abruptly or focusing on distractions: This behavior indicates a desire to avoid the conversation at hand and can be frustrating for the partner seeking open communication.

Emotional withdrawal:

- Shutting down emotionally: This involves refusing to acknowledge the other person's feelings, appearing cold and distant, and displaying a lack of empathy or interest in understanding their perspective.

- Stonewalling can manifest in subtle ways, making it crucial to be attentive to both verbal and non-verbal cues, as well as the overall emotional atmosphere of the interaction.

CHAPTER 4

THE IMPACT ON RELATIONSHIPS

The consequences of these behaviors can be significant and detrimental:

- Emotional manipulation: Both tactics are forms of emotional manipulation, using silence as a weapon to control and punish the other person. This can leave the receiving partner feeling hurt, confused, and controlled, questioning their own reality and self-worth.

- Erosion of trust: Withdrawing from communication creates a sense of distance and distrust, making it difficult for partners to feel safe and secure in the relationship. Open and honest communication is essential for building trust, and these behaviors chip away at its foundation.

- Unresolved conflicts: Issues remain unaddressed, festering beneath the surface and potentially escalating later. When problems aren't dealt with openly and honestly, they can grow larger and more complex over time.

- Withdrawal and disconnection: Communication breakdown leads to feelings of loneliness, disconnection, and a sense of emotional abandonment. The silence creates a barrier, pushing partners apart and hindering the emotional connection vital for a healthy relationship

WHAT TO DO WHEN FACED WITH SILENT TREATMENT AND STONEWALLING

Being on the receiving end of silent treatment or stonewalling can be a deeply unsettling and hurtful experience.

Here, we explore what it feels like, what to say (and what not to say), and how to navigate this emotionally charged situation:

The silence can evoke a range of negative emotions, including:

CHAPTER 4

- Hurt and confusion: The lack of communication leaves you feeling emotionally abandoned and unsure of what you did wrong.

- Frustration and anger: The withdrawal feels like a form of punishment, leaving you frustrated and at a loss for how to resolve the situation.

- Insecurity and self-doubt: You might question your own perceptions and wonder if you are overreacting or responsible for the silence.

- Loneliness and disconnection: The lack of emotional connection can leave you feeling isolated and alone in the relationship.

WHAT TO SAY

- Express your feelings using "I" statements: Instead of saying, "You're always shutting me out!", try, "I feel hurt and disconnected when we don't talk about things that are bothering you."

- Seek clarification in a calm and non-blaming way: Instead of saying, "Why are you being so cold?", try, "Are you open to talking about what's going on? I'm feeling like we're not connecting right now."

- Set boundaries: Instead of saying, "Please don't ever shut me out again!", try, "I need you to communicate with me, even if it's difficult. Silence makes me feel alone and unheard."

- Express empathy: Try to understand your partner's perspective and validate their feelings, even if you disagree with their actions. For example, "I can see that you're upset, and I want to understand what's bothering you."

- Offer support: Let your partner know that you're there for them and willing to listen whenever they're ready to talk. You can say, "I'm here to listen whenever you're ready to talk. We can work through this together."

WHAT NOT TO SAY AND DO

CHAPTER 4

- Accusatory statements: Instead of saying, "You're being childish by shutting down!", try focusing on expressing your feelings without blaming your partner.

- Threats or ultimatums: Instead of saying, "If you don't talk to me, I'm leaving!", avoid using threats that can further escalate the situation and hinder open communication.

- Begging or pleading: Instead of saying, "Please, just talk to me! I can't handle this silence!", avoid behaviors that reinforce the dynamic where your partner controls the communication flow through silence.

- Minimizing their feelings: Instead of saying, "You're overreacting, it's not a big deal," try to validate their emotions and show understanding. For example, "I can see that this is important to you, and I want to understand why."

- Ignoring their need for space: Instead of pressuring them to talk immediately, respect their boundaries and give them the time and space they need to process their emotions. Avoid pushing for conversation when they're not ready.

CHAPTER 4

STRATEGIES TO DEAL WITH SILENT TEATMENT AND STONEWALLING

- Recognize the Behavior: Acknowledge and accept that silent treatment and stonewalling are not healthy or productive ways to communicate. Understand the impact of these behaviors on your partner and the relationship.

- Identify Triggers: Reflect on the situations or topics that typically lead to your silent treatment or stonewalling behavior. Recognize your triggers and try to understand why they evoke such strong reactions.

- Practice Self-Awareness: Pay attention to your thoughts, feelings, and physical sensations when you feel the urge to engage in silent treatment or stonewalling. Identify any underlying emotions, such as anger, fear, or insecurity, driving your behavior.

- Communicate Your Needs: Instead of shutting down or withdrawing, express your feelings and needs to your partner in a constructive manner. Use "I" statements to communicate how you're feeling without blaming or criticizing them.

STRATEGIES TO DEAL WITH SILENT TEATMENT AND STONEWALLING

- Take Responsibility: Take ownership of your behavior and its impact on your partner and the relationship. Apologize for any hurt or distress caused by your silent treatment or stonewalling, and commit to finding healthier ways to communicate.

- Develop Coping Strategies: Find alternative ways to manage difficult emotions and cope with stress without resorting to silent treatment or stonewalling. Practice relaxation techniques, such as deep breathing or mindfulness, to calm your mind and body. Or engage in physical activity or exercise to release pent-up tension.

- Commit to Change: Make a conscious effort to change your communication patterns and replace silent treatment and stonewalling with more constructive approaches. Be patient with yourself as you work towards positive change and be open to feedback from your partner.

By implementing these strategies, you can take proactive steps to address silent treatment and stonewalling behavior and cultivate healthier and more effective communication in your relationship.

PHRASES TO SAY TO YOUR PARTNER WHEN YOU FEEL YOURSELF SHUTTING DOWN

- "I'm feeling overwhelmed right now, and I need some time to collect my thoughts."
- "I notice myself starting to withdraw, and I want to let you know what's going on."
- "I'm struggling to find the right words to express how I'm feeling."

CHAPTER 4

- "I'm feeling defensive, and I don't want to say something I might regret. Can we revisit this conversation later?"
- "I need a moment to process what you're saying before I respond."
- "I'm feeling triggered by this conversation, and I need a break to calm down."
- "I'm feeling myself shutting down, and I want to work on staying engaged in the conversation."
- "I'm feeling uncomfortable, and I need to take a step back to reflect on what's going on for me."
- "I'm struggling to stay present in this conversation, and I want to address that before we continue."
- "I'm noticing myself withdrawing, and I want to find a way to stay connected with you."

Using these phrases can help you communicate your internal experiences to your partner and take proactive steps to prevent full shutdown or stonewalling during difficult conversations.

WORKSHEET

REFLECTIVE QUESTIONS

- Why do I resort to giving the silent treatment when faced with conflict or discomfort?
- How do I justify my silence to myself in the moment? What beliefs or thoughts support this behavior?
- What emotions am I trying to avoid or protect myself from by remaining silent?
- How does my silent treatment impact my partner and our relationship dynamics?
- Have I observed this behavior in others or learned it from past experiences? If so, what can I learn from those instances?
- What underlying fears or insecurities might be driving my tendency to shut down during difficult conversations?
- What do I hope to achieve or gain by giving the silent treatment? Is this approach effective in achieving those goals?
- How do I feel about the long-term effects of my silent treatment on my relationship and my partner's well-being

WORKSHEET

- Are there alternative ways I could express my needs, emotions, or boundaries that would be more constructive and respectful?

- What steps can I take to break the cycle of silent treatment and cultivate healthier communication habits in my relationship?

NOTES

NOTES

NOTES

NOTES

CHAPTER 5

"Passive aggression is the weapon of choice for those afraid to confront their true feelings."

– Unknown –

CHAPTER 5

Healthy relationships rely on clear and direct communication. However, sometimes negativity creeps in through a more subtle route: passive-aggressive behavior.

Passive-aggressive behavior can be as perplexing as it is frustrating. It involves expressing negativity indirectly, often through veiled comments, sarcasm, or through withholding cooperation.

Unlike the outright hostility of yelling or name-calling, passive-aggressive behavior leaves the recipient confused, unsure of how to respond, and ultimately, hurt and disrespected.

In this chapter, we'll unveil the complexities of passive-aggressive behavior, exploring its causes, the emotional toll it takes on relationships, and most importantly, how to confront it constructively for a healthier dynamic.

UNDERSTANDING PASSIVE-AGGRESSION

CHAPTER 5

Passive aggression is a behavior characterized by indirect resistance to the demands or expectations of others. Instead of openly expressing their feelings or needs, individuals may resort to subtle, non-verbal, or passive means of communication.

This can include sarcasm, avoidance, procrastination, or intentionally neglecting responsibilities.

COMMON TRIGGERS OF PASSIVE AGGRESSION

Common triggers of passive aggression in romantic relationships can vary depending on the individual and the dynamics of the relationship. However, some common triggers may include:

- Unmet Expectations: When one partner's expectations are not fulfilled, they may resort to passive-aggressive behavior as a way to express their disappointment or frustration indirectly.

CHAPTER 5

- Feeling Disrespected or Disregarded: Perceived disrespect or disregard for one's feelings or opinions can trigger passive-aggressive responses, such as giving the silent treatment or making sarcastic remarks.

- Fear of Rejection: Fear of rejection or abandonment can lead to passive-aggressive behavior as individuals may struggle to express their needs or desires openly, fearing rejection or disapproval from their partner.

- Power Struggles: Power struggles within the relationship, such as disagreements over decision-making or control, can trigger passive-aggressive behavior as individuals vie for control or dominance in the relationship.

- Emotional Insecurity: Feelings of insecurity or inadequacy can trigger passive-aggressive responses, as individuals may use indirect means to assert themselves or protect themselves from vulnerability.

- Conflict Avoidance: Individuals who avoid conflict or confrontation may resort to passive aggression as a way to express their dissatisfaction or anger without directly addressing the issue.

CHAPTER 5

- Communication Breakdown: Poor communication or misunderstandings can lead to passive-aggressive behavior as individuals struggle to express themselves effectively or feel misunderstood by their partner.

HIDDEN PAINS BEHIND PASSIVE AGGRESSION

Hidden pains associated with passive-aggressive behavior in romantic relationships include:

- Unresolved Resentment: Passive-aggressive behavior can stem from unresolved resentment or anger towards a partner, often rooted in past conflicts or unmet expectations.

- Fear of Confrontation: Individuals may resort to passive aggression as a coping mechanism to avoid direct confrontation, fearing the potential for conflict or rejection.

CHAPTER 5

- Lack of Communication Skills: Difficulty expressing emotions or needs openly and assertively can lead to passive-aggressive behavior as individuals struggle to communicate effectively with their partner.

- Low Self-Esteem: Feelings of inadequacy or low self-worth may contribute to passive-aggressive behavior, as individuals may use indirect means to assert control or gain a sense of power in the relationship.

- Avoidance of Vulnerability: Passive aggression can serve as a defense mechanism to protect oneself from vulnerability, allowing individuals to maintain emotional distance and avoid intimacy with their partner.

- Insecurity and Jealousy: Feelings of insecurity or jealousy may manifest as passive-aggressive behavior, such as making sarcastic remarks or giving the silent treatment, as a way to express dissatisfaction or seek attention.

- Control Issues: Passive-aggressive behavior can also be driven by a desire for control or manipulation within the relationship, as individuals attempt to assert influence or dominance without directly addressing their needs or desires.

EXAMPLES OF PASSIVE AGGRESSION

Passive-aggressive behavior manifests in various ways, often leaving the target feeling like they're "walking on eggshells." Here are some common examples, along with their underlying intent and potential impact:

- Backhanded compliments: (e.g., "That outfit looks...interesting on you." said with a sarcastic tone). This seemingly positive statement actually conveys criticism or disapproval in a disguised manner. It can leave the recipient feeling belittled and unsure of how to respond, creating confusion and hurt.

CHAPTER 5

- The silent treatment: (e.g., withdrawing from communication or giving one-word responses to express displeasure). This behavior aims to punish or control the other person by withholding communication. It creates emotional distance, disconnection, and can leave the recipient feeling ignored and unimportant.

- Feigning forgetfulness: (e.g., "Oh, I forgot to do that chore we talked about again..." said in a nonchalant way). This passive-aggressive tactic involves deliberately neglecting a responsibility or task, often communicated through a casual or even playful tone. It can breed resentment and frustration in the recipient, who feels burdened and disrespected.

- Sulking or pouting: Using nonverbal cues like pouting, crossed arms, or facial expressions to express disapproval without directly communicating the issue. This non-verbal form of passive-aggression leaves the recipient to interpret the message, leading to confusion and emotional manipulation.

- Procrastination or inefficiency: (e.g., deliberately delaying tasks or completing them poorly as a form of passive resistance). This involves intentionally putting off or performing tasks in a subpar manner to express dissent or frustration. It can hinder progress, create additional work for others, and ultimately sabotage the relationship's well-being.

EXAMPLES OF PASSIVE AGGRESSION

Passive-aggressive behaviors can have a significant negative impact on relationships, both in the short and long term:

- Creates confusion and resentment: The indirect nature of passive-aggressive communication leaves the recipient unsure of the true message and the sender's intent. This ambiguity can lead to confusion, frustration, and resentment, as the recipient tries to decipher the hidden meaning and feels manipulated by the lack of direct communication.

- Erodes trust and intimacy: Withholding honest communication creates a sense of distance and distrust. It hinders emotional intimacy as partners are unable to openly express their feelings and needs, creating barriers to connection and vulnerability.

- Breeds negativity and hostility: Unresolved negativity from passive-aggressive behaviors can create a hostile environment within the relationship. The indirect expression of anger and frustration can build up over time, poisoning the atmosphere and making it difficult for partners to feel comfortable and secure.

- Hinders problem-solving: Indirect communication makes it difficult to address issues directly and collaboratively. Without open and honest communication, genuine understanding and effective problem-solving are hampered, leaving issues unresolved and potentially escalating over time.

ON THE RECEIVING END OF PASSIVE AGGRESSIVE BEHAVIOR?

CHAPTER 5

Being the target of passive-aggressive behavior can be a frustrating and emotionally draining experience.

Here's what it might feel like and how to navigate this situation:

- The Emotional Rollercoaster: You might experience a range of emotions, including confusion, hurt, anger, and frustration. The indirect nature of the behavior makes it difficult to understand the true message, leaving you feeling unsure of how to respond.

- Self-Doubt and Blame: You might question your own perceptions and wonder if you're overreacting. The manipulative nature of passive-aggression can make you feel like you're the one causing the problem, leading to self-doubt and unnecessary blame.

- Feeling Disconnected and Isolated: The lack of open communication creates a sense of emotional distance and disconnection. It can be difficult to feel close and trusting when your partner is unwilling to communicate directly.

CHAPTER 5

- Walking on Eggshells: You might feel constantly on guard, unsure of what will trigger the next passive-aggressive behavior. This can create a tense and stressful environment within the relationship.

HOW TO RESPOND (AND NOT REACT)

While it's natural to feel frustrated or angry, reacting impulsively can escalate the situation. Here are some strategies to respond effectively:

- Don't take the bait: Recognize the passive-aggressive behavior for what it is and avoid getting drawn into an emotional reaction. Take a deep breath and try to stay calm.

- Seek clarification: In a calm and assertive way, try to understand the underlying message. You can say something like, "I'm not sure I understand what you're trying to say. Can you rephrase that?"

CHAPTER 5

- Set boundaries: Communicate that you expect open and honest communication in the relationship. Let your partner know how their behavior is affecting you.

- Focus on "I" statements: Instead of accusatory statements, express your feelings using "I" statements. For example, "I feel hurt when you say things like that." This helps your partner understand your perspective without putting them on the defensive.

REMEMBER

- You can't control your partner's behavior, but you can control your own. Focus on responding in a healthy way and communicating your needs clearly.

- Don't accept unhealthy communication patterns. If your partner is unwilling to change, it might be necessary to seek professional help or consider whether the relationship can be sustained.

CHAPTER 5

STRATEGIES FOR OVERCOMING PASSIVE AGGRESSION

Overcoming passive-aggressive behavior can be challenging, but with self-awareness and effort, individuals can learn to communicate more directly and assertively.

Here are some strategies for a person who behaves passive-aggressively to overcome their behavior:

- Increase Self-Awareness: Take time to reflect on your thoughts, feelings, and behaviors to recognize when you are engaging in passive-aggressive tendencies. Pay attention to patterns or triggers that lead to passive-aggressive responses.

- Practice Open Communication: Instead of resorting to indirect or passive-aggressive behavior, communicate your thoughts, feelings, and needs openly and directly with your partner. Use assertive communication techniques to express yourself clearly and respectfully.

- Address Underlying Emotions: **Explore the underlying emotions, such as anger, frustration, or fear, that may be driving your passive-aggressive behavior. Take steps to address these emotions in healthy ways, such as through journaling, therapy, or talking to a trusted friend or partner.**

- Take Responsibility: **Acknowledge your role in perpetuating passive-aggressive behavior and take responsibility for your actions. Avoid making excuses or blaming others for your behavior, and commit to making positive changes.**

- Practice Empathy: **Put yourself in your partner's shoes and consider how your passive-aggressive behavior may impact them. Cultivate empathy and understanding for their perspective, and strive to communicate with compassion and empathy.**

- Develop Conflict Resolution Skills: **Learn effective conflict resolution skills to address disagreements or conflicts in a constructive manner. Practice active listening, compromise, and problem-solving techniques to find mutually beneficial solutions.**

WORKSHEET

REFLECTIVE QUESTIONS

- Identifying Triggers: What situations or behaviors typically trigger you to resort to passive-aggressive communication? (e.g., feeling unheard, experiencing conflict, feeling overwhelmed)

- Recognizing Your Behavior: Reflect on recent interactions where you might have displayed passive-aggressive behavior. List examples of specific actions or behaviors you used. (e.g., giving backhanded compliments, using the silent treatment, procrastinating on tasks)

- Examining the Impact: Consider the impact your passive-aggressive behaviors have on others and your relationships. (e.g., confusion, frustration, resentment, distance)

- Underlying Emotions: What emotions are you typically feeling when you resort to passive-aggressive communication? (e.g., anger, frustration, hurt, fear)

WORKSHEET

- **Healthy Alternatives:** For each trigger find healthy and assertive communication strategies you can use instead of resorting to passive-aggression. (e.g., expressing your needs directly using "I" statements, taking a time-out to cool down before a conversation)

- **"I" Statements:** Practice formulating "I" statements to express your needs and feelings in a non-blaming way. Here are some examples: "I feel frustrated when..." instead of giving someone the silent treatment. "I need some time to cool down before we continue this conversation..." instead of pouting or sulking. "I would appreciate it if..." instead of making a backhanded compliment.

- **Active Listening:** When having a conversation, actively listen to the other person. This includes maintaining eye contact, summarizing what you hear, and asking clarifying questions.

Passive-aggressive behavior, while often unintentional, can have a detrimental impact on your relationships.

WORKSHEET

By recognizing the triggers that lead you to these behaviors, understanding the emotions behind them, and practicing healthier communication strategies, you can break the cycle and build stronger, more fulfilling connections.

Remember, open and honest communication, even when faced with difficult emotions, is key to fostering trust, intimacy, and a healthy relationship dynamic.

In the next chapter, we'll delve into Criticism and Contempt. While healthy communication is essential for thriving relationships, navigating criticism and contempt can be particularly challenging.

Criticism, when delivered constructively, can offer valuable feedback for growth. However, when delivered harshly or laced with contempt, it can become destructive and damaging to the relationship.

We delve into the complexities of criticism and contempt, exploring healthy ways to offer and receive feedback, and strategies to manage contempt effectively for a more respectful and nurturing relationship dynamic.

NOTES

NOTES

NOTES

NOTES

CHAPTER 6

"Criticism, like rain, should be gentle enough to nourish a man's
growth without destroying his roots."

- Frank A. Clark -

CHAPTER 6

Healthy relationships involve open communication, which can include offering and receiving feedback. However, navigating criticism and contempt can be a minefield.

While constructive criticism can offer a valuable tool for growth, it can easily turn destructive when delivered harshly or laced with contempt.

This chapter explores the complexities of these concepts, equipping you with strategies to effectively manage both and maintain a respectful and nurturing relationship dynamic.

UNDERSTANDING CRITICISM

Criticism involves expressing disapproval or judgment about someone's behavior, actions, or qualities. It may focus on specific behaviors or actions rather than attacking the person's character.

CHAPTER 6

Constructive criticism aims to provide feedback that can lead to improvement or growth. It typically involves offering specific suggestions or alternatives for change.

Criticism can be detrimental to relationships due to its tendency to erode trust, connection, and emotional well-being.

Constant criticism can lead to feelings of resentment, decreased self-esteem, and a lack of respect between partners. It often escalates conflict, hindering effective communication and making it difficult to address issues constructively.

While feedback is necessary for growth, relentless criticism delivered in a harsh or disrespectful manner can create a toxic atmosphere, ultimately undermining the foundation of the relationship.

Therefore, it's essential for partners to communicate with empathy, respect, and a focus on finding solutions rather than assigning blame.

CHAPTER 6

UNDERSTANDING CONTEMPT

Contempt goes beyond criticism and involves a deeper level of disdain or disrespect toward someone. It often reflects a feeling of superiority or moral judgment over the other person.

Contemptuous behavior can include mockery, sarcasm, name-calling, or belittling remarks. Unlike constructive criticism, contempt is more focused on attacking the person's character or worth rather than addressing specific behaviors.

Contempt is harmful in relationships because it conveys a profound lack of respect and empathy towards the other person. When one partner feels contempt for the other, it creates a toxic atmosphere characterized by disdain, superiority, and hostility.

Contemptuous behavior often includes insults, mockery, sarcasm, or belittling remarks, which can deeply wound the other person emotionally. This erodes trust and connection, leading to feelings of resentment, hurt, and worthlessness.

CHAPTER 6

Over time, contempt can escalate conflict and deteriorate communication, making it nearly impossible to resolve issues or maintain a healthy relationship.

Ultimately, contempt undermines the foundation of mutual respect, empathy, and understanding that is essential for a thriving partnership.

COMMON TRIGGERS OF CRITICISM AND CONTEMPT

- Unmet Expectations: When one partner feels that their expectations are not being met, they may resort to criticism or contempt as a way to express frustration or disappointment.

- Perceived Threats to Self-Esteem: Criticism and contempt can arise when one partner feels threatened or insecure about their self-worth or identity within the relationship. This can occur if they perceive criticism from their partner as a personal attack on their competence or character.

CHAPTER 6

- Communication Breakdown: Poor communication or misunderstandings can contribute to criticism and contempt. When partners feel unheard or misunderstood, they may become resentful and express their frustrations through criticism or contemptuous behavior.

- Built-Up Resentment: Unresolved conflicts or recurring issues that have not been addressed can lead to built-up resentment over time. This resentment may manifest as criticism or contempt towards the other partner.

- Power Imbalance: Power imbalances within the relationship, such as one partner exerting control or dominance over the other, can trigger feelings of resentment and provoke criticism or contemptuous behavior.

- Stress and External Pressures: External stressors such as financial difficulties, work-related stress, or family issues can increase tension within the relationship and contribute to criticism and contempt.

- Lack of Emotional Connection: When partners feel disconnected emotionally, they may resort to criticism or contempt as a way to express their dissatisfaction or to seek attention from their partner.

HIDDEN PAIN BEHIND CRITICISM AND CONTEMPT

Behind criticism and contempt, there can be hidden pains and unresolved emotions that contribute to these behaviors:

- Insecurity: Criticism and contempt may stem from feelings of insecurity within oneself or the relationship. Individuals who feel inadequate or uncertain about their own worth may project these feelings onto their partner through criticism or contemptuous behavior.

- Fear of Rejection or Abandonment: Criticism and contempt can also be driven by a fear of rejection or abandonment. Individuals may use these behaviors as a defense mechanism to push their partner away or to test their loyalty and commitment.

- Past Trauma: Hidden pains from past experiences, such as childhood trauma or previous relationships, can influence how individuals express themselves in their current relationship. Criticism and contempt may be rooted in unresolved issues from the past that are triggered by present-day events or interactions.

- Unmet Emotional Needs: When emotional needs are not being met within the relationship, individuals may express their frustration or longing through criticism or contempt. These behaviors may be an attempt to communicate underlying feelings of loneliness, neglect, or longing for connection.

- Loss of Control: Criticism and contempt can also arise from a sense of loss of control or power within the relationship. Individuals may use these behaviors as a way to regain a sense of control or to assert dominance over their partner.

EXAMPLES OF CONTEMPT

CHAPTER 6

- Eye-rolling or sneering when your partner speaks.
- Making sarcastic remarks or mocking your partner's opinions or actions.
- Belittling your partner's achievements or abilities.
- Using derogatory nicknames or insults to address your partner.
- Dismissing your partner's feelings or opinions as irrelevant or silly.
- Expressing disgust or disdain towards your partner's habits or interests.
- Ignoring your partner's attempts to communicate or connect emotionally.
- Physically turning away or avoiding your partner during conversations or interactions.

EXAMPLES OF CRITICISM

- "You always forget to do the dishes. You're so lazy."
- "Why can't you be more like [someone else]? They're always so thoughtful and considerate."
- "You never listen to me. It's like talking to a brick wall."
- "You're terrible with money. I can't trust you to handle our finances."

- "You're so selfish. You never think about anyone but yourself."
- "You're such a failure. I don't know why I even bother trying to talk to you."
- "You're so disorganized. I can't rely on you to keep anything in order."
- "You're always interrupting me. Can't you just let me finish my sentence for once?"

THE DEVASTATING IMPACT OF CRITICISM AND CONTEMPT:

Contempt can have a profound and lasting negative impact on relationships, leading to a cascade of problems:

- Emotional withdrawal: Feeling attacked and disrespected can lead partners to emotionally withdraw from the relationship, creating distance and hindering intimacy.

- Increased defensiveness: When feeling belittled or attacked, individuals might become defensive and resistant to any feedback, even if it is constructive. This can create a cycle of negativity and hinder effective communication.

- Escalating conflict: Contempt, by its very nature, fuels negativity and hostility. When contempt becomes entrenched in a relationship, it can escalate even minor disagreements into full-blown conflicts, making it difficult to resolve issues constructively.

- Erosion of trust and intimacy: Trust and intimacy are the cornerstones of healthy relationships. When contempt becomes the norm, these vital elements gradually erode, leaving partners feeling insecure, disconnected, and unable to fully trust or open up to each other.

WHAT ABOUT THE PERSON ON THE RECEIVING END?

Being on the receiving end can deeply impact your self-esteem and emotional stability, leading to feelings of inadequacy and strain in your relationship.

Here's what it might feel like:

- Hurt and Rejection: Contemptuous behavior and critical remarks can deeply wound emotionally, leading to feelings of hurt, rejection, and worthlessness.

- Anger and Resentment: Being subjected to contempt and criticism can provoke anger and resentment towards the partner who displays such behaviors, creating tension and animosity in the relationship.

- Defensiveness and Withdrawal: Contempt and criticism often trigger defensiveness as the person seeks to protect themselves from further emotional harm. This can lead to avoidance of certain interactions or emotional withdrawal from the relationship.

- Inadequacy and Self-Doubt: Constant criticism can erode self-esteem and confidence, fostering feelings of inadequacy and self-doubt as the person internalizes negative feedback and questions their own worth.

CHAPTER 6

When addressing criticism and contempt behavior in a partner, it's crucial to avoid blaming or attacking them, as this can escalate conflict and further damage the relationship.

Instead, focus on expressing your feelings, setting boundaries, and working together to find constructive solutions.

PHRASES TO USE WHEN YOUR PARTNER IS CRITISIZING YOU

When you notice your partner criticizing you, it's important to address the issue calmly and assertively while maintaining respect for both yourself and your partner.

Here are some more phrases you can use:

- "I feel hurt when I hear criticism from you. Can we talk about this?"
- "I understand you might have concerns, but I'd appreciate it if we could discuss them without criticism."

CHAPTER 6

- "I value your feedback, but I'm finding it challenging to handle constant criticism. Can we find a more constructive way to communicate?"
- "It seems like we're focusing on the negatives. Can we also talk about the positives and how we can support each other?"
- "I want us to communicate openly and respectfully. Can we agree to express our concerns without resorting to criticism?"
- "I'm open to feedback, but it's important to me that it's delivered respectfully. Can we find a better way to communicate our concerns?"
- "When you criticize me, it makes me feel defensive. Let's find a way to address issues without putting each other down."

WHAT NOT TO SAY

- "You're always so critical and disrespectful. Why can't you change?"
- "I can't believe you said that. You're so contemptuous!"

CHAPTER 6

- "You're the problem in our relationship. If you could just stop being so critical, everything would be fine."
- "I don't want to hear your criticisms anymore. Just keep your opinions to yourself."
- "You're just like [negative comparison]. I can't stand your behavior."

STRATEGIES FOR OVERCOMING CRITICISM AND CONTEMPT

If you find yourself struggling with feelings of contempt towards your partner, it's crucial to address the issue head-on. Here are some strategies to help you manage contempt and build a healthier relationship dynamic:

- Reflect on Your Behavior: Take time to reflect on your own actions and words. Recognize when you're being critical or contemptuous towards your partner and try to understand the underlying reasons for your behavior.

CHAPTER 6

- Identify Triggers: Pay attention to the situations or behaviors that trigger your criticism and contempt. Understanding your triggers can help you develop strategies to manage your reactions more effectively.

- Practice Empathy: Put yourself in your partner's shoes and try to understand their perspective. Consider how your criticism and contempt may be impacting them emotionally and the dynamics of your relationship.

- Communicate Effectively: Instead of resorting to criticism or contemptuous behavior, communicate your feelings and needs assertively and respectfully. Use "I" statements to express yourself and avoid blaming or attacking your partner.

- Focus on Solutions: Shift your focus from criticizing your partner to finding constructive solutions to any issues or conflicts that arise in the relationship. Collaborate with your partner to address concerns and work towards mutual goals.

CHAPTER 6

- Practice Self-Care: Take care of yourself physically, emotionally, and mentally. Engage in activities that help you relax and manage stress effectively, such as exercise, meditation, or hobbies.

- Be Patient and Persistent: Overcoming criticism and contempt takes time and effort. Be patient with yourself and your partner as you work towards positive changes in your behavior and relationship dynamics.

WORKSHEET

REFLECTIVE QUESTIONS

- Identifying Triggers: **What situations or behaviors typically trigger you to criticize or show contempt towards your partner? (e.g., feeling unappreciated, experiencing stress, perceiving failure). Reflect on past interactions where you felt compelled to criticize or show contempt. What specific circumstances or behaviors tend to provoke these reactions?**

- Recognizing Your Behavior: **Can you recall recent instances where you criticized or showed contempt towards your partner? Describe specific actions or behaviors you exhibited during these interactions. (e.g., making derogatory remarks, belittling achievements, expressing disdain) How do you typically express criticism or contempt towards your partner? Are there patterns or recurring behaviors you notice in your communication?**

WORKSHEET

- **Examining the Impact:** Consider the impact your criticism and contempt have on your partner and your relationship. How do these behaviors affect your partner's emotional well-being and the dynamics of your relationship? Reflect on any feedback or reactions you've received from your partner regarding your criticism and contempt. How do their responses make you feel?

- **Underlying Emotions:** What emotions are typically present when you resort to criticizing or showing contempt towards your partner? (e.g., frustration, resentment, insecurity, disappointment). Are there underlying feelings or needs that drive your criticism and contempt? (e.g., a desire for control, fear of inadequacy, unresolved past issues)

- **Healthy Alternatives:** For each trigger, brainstorm healthy and assertive communication strategies you can use instead of resorting to criticism and contempt. (e.g., expressing appreciation, discussing concerns calmly, validating your partner's feelings). How can you cultivate empathy and understanding towards your partner's perspective, even in challenging situations?

WORKSHEET

Navigating criticism and contempt can be challenging, but by developing effective communication skills and addressing the underlying causes of these issues, you can foster a relationship built on respect, empathy, and understanding.

Remember, open and honest communication, even when faced with difficult situations, is the cornerstone of healthy relationships.

By learning to deliver and receive feedback constructively, you can create a space for growth and strengthen the foundation of your partnership.

The next chapter is all about conflict resolution. Conflict is an inevitable part of any relationship. Differences in opinion, unmet needs, and external stressors can all contribute to disagreements and arguments.

While conflict can be disruptive, it also presents an opportunity for growth and a deeper understanding of your partner.

WORKSHEET

This chapter dives into the complexities of conflict resolution, equipping you with tools and strategies to navigate disagreements constructively, strengthen your communication skills, and emerge from conflict feeling closer and more connected than ever before.

NOTES

NOTES

NOTES

NOTES

NOTES

CHAPTER 7

"The goal of resolving conflict in a relationship is not victory or defeat. It's reaching understanding and letting go of our need to be right."

- Unknown -

CHAPTER 7

Conflict is an inevitable part of any relationship, not a reason to sound the alarm bells. In fact, navigating conflict constructively can be a potent catalyst for growth, deeper understanding, and strengthening your bond as a couple.

This chapter equips you with tools and strategies to transform conflict from a battleground into a space for collaboration, connection, and building a more fulfilling relationship.

UNDERSTANDING CONFLICT BETWEEN COUPLES

- Sources of Conflict: Identifying common triggers that ignite the flames of conflict, such as:

  - Unmet Needs: When needs for connection, respect, intimacy, or security are not met consistently, resentment and frustration can build, leading to conflict.

- Communication breakdowns: Ineffective communication, including poor listening skills, unclear expressions, and resorting to blame instead of understanding, can fuel misunderstandings and conflict

- Personality differences: While opposites can attract, clashing communication styles, values, or expectations based on individual personalities can lead to disagreements and conflict.

- External stressors: External factors like work stress, financial difficulties, or family issues can add strain to a relationship and contribute to conflict.

- Unresolved emotional baggage: Past hurts, unresolved emotional issues, and unaddressed traumas can resurface and manifest in conflicts if not addressed constructively.

- The Impact of Conflict: Exploring the potential positive and negative outcomes of conflict:

Positive outcomes:

- Growth: **Navigating conflict constructively can lead to personal and relational growth by fostering self-awareness, improving communication skills, and strengthening problem-solving abilities.**

- Deeper understanding: **Open and honest communication during conflict can lead to a deeper understanding of your partner's needs, perspectives, and triggers.**

- Strengthened communication: **Engaging in healthy conflict resolution practices can strengthen your communication skills and equip you to address future disagreements more effectively.**

Negative outcomes:

- Resentment and disconnection: **Unresolved conflicts can lead to feelings of resentment, anger, and disconnection, eroding the emotional foundation of the relationship.**

o Emotional distress: Conflict, especially when handled ineffectively, can cause significant emotional distress for both partners, leading to anxiety, depression, and feelings of isolation.

o Relationship breakdown: Unmanaged conflict can ultimately lead to a breakdown in the relationship if left unaddressed.

EFFECTIVE COMMUNICATION TECHNIQUES FOR RESOLVING CONFLICTS

The cornerstone of healthy conflict resolution lies in effective communication. Here are key techniques to adopt:

- Active Listening: This goes beyond simply hearing your partner's words. It involves:

  o Paying close attention: Maintain eye contact, minimize distractions, and avoid interrupting.

- Reflecting back: Summarize what you heard and clarify your understanding to avoid misunderstandings.

- Validating their feelings: Acknowledge their emotions without judgment, even if you disagree with their perspective.

- Assertiveness: Expressing your needs and feelings honestly and directly, while respecting your partner's thoughts and feelings. Assertiveness involves:

  - "I" statements: Owning your feelings and taking responsibility for your perspective. (e.g., "I feel hurt when..." instead of "You always...")

  - Clear and direct communication: Expressing your needs and desires clearly, avoiding vagueness or passive-aggressive behavior.

  - Respectful and confident: Delivering your message with respect for your partner and confidence in your own needs and perspectives.

- Nonviolent Communication (NVC): This framework helps communicate effectively and avoid blame, focusing on four key elements:

  - Observation: Describe the situation objectively without judgment. (e.g., "I see that the dishes haven't been done again.")

  - Feelings: Express your own feelings associated with the situation. (e.g., "I feel frustrated because...")

  - Needs: Identify the underlying needs that are not being met. (e.g., "I need help with keeping the house clean.")

  - Requests: Clearly state a specific request for your partner, focusing on a solution. (e.g., "Would you be willing to help with the dishes in the future?")

CONFLICT RESOLUTION STRATEGIES

CHAPTER 7

Moving beyond effective communication, various strategies can equip you to navigate and resolve conflicts constructively:

Collaborative Problem-Solving Approaches

- *Negotiation:* This approach involves finding mutually agreeable solutions through open communication and compromise. Here are key aspects:

  - *Identify common ground:* Seek areas of agreement and shared interests to build upon.

  - *Brainstorm solutions:* Explore various options together and be open to creative solutions that address both partners' needs.

  - *Compromise:* Be willing to give and take to reach a solution that satisfies both parties to a reasonable extent.

TECHNIQUES FOR DE-ESCALATING CONFLICTS AND MANAGING EMOTIONS

- Taking time-outs: Allowing both partners to cool down and regain emotional control before continuing the conversation is crucial. This prevents further escalation and allows for more rational and constructive communication when you resume the conversation.

- Focusing on the present: Avoid bringing up past grievances or dwelling on hurt feelings. By staying focused on the current issue and avoiding unproductive blame games, you can navigate the conflict more effectively.

PHRASES TO STOP AN ARGUMENT IN ITS TRACKS

While the heat of the moment might make it challenging, having a few pre-determined phrases can help de-escalate a situation:

CHAPTER 7

- "I need a time-out to calm down. Can we continue this conversation later?"

- "I hear you're upset. Can you help me understand how I'm making you feel?"

- "I understand your perspective. What can we do to find a solution that works for both of us?"

ACKNOWLEDGING AND VALIDATING

- "I understand you're feeling frustrated right now. Can we talk about this when we've both calmed down?"

- "It sounds like this is a big issue for you. Let's take some time to breathe and then come back to it with a clear head."

- "I can see why you're upset. What can I do to help the situation?"

CHAPTER 7

SEEKING CLARIFICATION AND TAKING RESPONSIBILITY

- "Can you help me understand why you're feeling this way?" (Shows willingness to see their perspective)

- "Maybe I wasn't clear enough before. What I meant was..." (Takes ownership of communication breakdown)

- "Is there something specific I did that's bothering you?" (Allows for pinpointing the issue)

SUGGESTING SOLUTIONS AND COLLABORATION

- "Let's take a step back and brainstorm some solutions together."

- "Is there something I can do differently moving forward?" (Shows willingness to adapt)

- "What would a solution look like for you?" (Focuses on finding common ground)

SHIFTING FOCUS AND TAKING A BREAK

- "Maybe we should revisit this later when we've had some time to think about it."

- "This conversation seems to be getting heated. Can we take a break and come back to it later?"

- "I'd love to keep talking about this, but right now I need some space to cool down. How about we pick this up in an hour?" (Sets a clear boundary)

HUMOR (USE WITH CAUTION)

- "Woah, hold on there! Let's not let this turn into a full-blown movie scene, okay?" (Can lighten the mood if appropriate)

- "If this were a sitcom, I'd say it's time for a commercial break. Let's take a breather."

- "Looks like we stumbled into a rom-com plot. Time to fast-forward to the happy ending."

CHAPTER 7

Remember, these are not magic bullets, but rather tools to nudge the conversation back to a place of constructive dialogue.

WORKSHEET

REFLECTIVE QUESTIONS

- "What patterns do I notice in my communication style during conflicts or disagreements?"
- "How do my communication habits impact my relationships with others, both positively and negatively?"
- "What emotions typically arise for me during difficult conversations, and how do they influence my responses?"
- "What fears or insecurities might be underlying my defensive, passive-aggressive, or critical behaviors?"
- "How do I typically respond when I feel criticized or challenged? Is this response serving me and my relationships well?"
- "What communication techniques or strategies have I found effective in diffusing conflicts or improving understanding?"
- "What values do I want to embody in my communication with others, and how can I align my actions with those values?"
- "How do I handle disagreements or differing opinions, and are there ways I could approach them more constructively?"

WORKSHEET

- "What steps can I take to cultivate a more supportive and respectful communication style in my relationships?"

By understanding the sources of conflict, employing effective communication techniques, and utilizing conflict resolution strategies, you can transform conflicts into opportunities for growth and deeper connection.

Remember, navigating conflict ethically, acknowledging power dynamics, and fostering mutual respect are essential for building a strong and fulfilling relationship.

As you embark on this journey of navigating conflict, remember that personal growth is equally important.

In the next chapter, we're diving into something pretty special: emotional connection. It's that intangible spark that makes relationships feel alive and vibrant.

We'll explore what it means to truly connect with someone on an emotional level and how it can transform the way we relate to others.

Are you ready for the final chapter?

NOTES

NOTES

NOTES

NOTES

NOTES

CHAPTER 8

"Emotional connection is the heartbeat of a thriving relationship, where words often fail but hearts understand."

- Unknown -

CHAPTER 8

In this chapter, we delve into the profound significance of emotional connection in couples communication. We explore how fostering a strong emotional bond enhances communication, deepens intimacy, and strengthens the overall health of the relationship.

Here are some key aspects of emotional connection:

- Intimacy: This involves sharing your thoughts, feelings, and experiences with your partner in a safe and supportive space. It allows you to be vulnerable and open up without fear of judgment.

- Empathy: This is the ability to understand and share the feelings of your partner. It involves putting yourself in their shoes and seeing things from their perspective.

- Trust: This is the foundation of a healthy emotional connection. It allows you to feel safe and secure with your partner, knowing they will be there for you and have your best interests at heart.

CHAPTER 8

- Vulnerability: This involves being open and honest with your partner, even about your flaws and insecurities. It allows you to build a deeper connection by showing your authentic self.

- Shared values and goals: Having a sense of common ground and shared aspirations can strengthen the emotional connection in a relationship.

WHAT EMOTIONAL CONNECTION LOOKS LIKE

- Feeling comfortable enough to talk to your partner about anything, even difficult topics.

- Feeling supported and understood by your partner during challenging times.

- Feeling a sense of joy and connection when you're together, even when doing simple things.

- Being able to celebrate each other's successes and offer comfort during times of sadness.

- Feeling a sense of security and stability in the relationship.

THE IMPORTANCE OF EMOTIONAL CONNECTION

Emotional connection acts as the lifeblood of healthy, fulfilling relationships. It's more than just feeling good around someone; it's a deep and meaningful bond built on trust, empathy, vulnerability, and a sense of being truly understood and valued. Here's why emotional connection is so important:

Benefits for the Individual:

- Increased Happiness and Well-being: Feeling connected to another person provides a sense of security, belonging, and purpose. This sense of support can significantly boost your overall happiness and well-being.

CHAPTER 8

- Enhanced Emotional Regulation: Sharing your feelings and experiences with a supportive partner allows you to process emotions more effectively. This can lead to better emotional regulation and a stronger sense of self.

- Improved Self-Esteem: Feeling seen, heard, and appreciated for who you are can significantly boost your self-esteem.

- Reduced Stress and Anxiety: Emotional connection provides a safe space to share burdens and anxieties, lessening their impact on your mental health.

Benefits for the Relationship:

- Stronger Foundation: Emotional connection lays the groundwork for a strong and lasting relationship. It allows you to weather life's challenges together and emerge even stronger.

- Improved Communication: Feeling safe and understood fosters open and honest communication. This allows you to address disagreements constructively and build trust over time.

CHAPTER 8

- Deeper Intimacy: Emotional connection allows you to build intimacy beyond the physical. It fosters a sense of closeness and connection on a deeper emotional level.

- Increased Conflict Resolution: Feeling connected makes you more likely to approach conflict with empathy and understanding, leading to quicker and more constructive resolution.

Overall Impact:

Emotional connection creates a positive ripple effect throughout your life and relationship.

It creates a safe space for growth, fosters resilience, and allows you to experience the joys of love and connection on a deeper level.

It's not always easy, and it requires effort from both partners, but the benefits of emotional connection make it a worthwhile pursuit for all involved.

CHAPTER 8

DAILY AND WEEKLY PRACTICES FOR COUPLES

Building and maintaining emotional connection requires conscious effort and consistent nurturing. Here are some ideas for fostering emotional connection on a daily and weekly basis:

Daily Practices:

- **Small Gestures of Affection:** Show your partner you care through small acts of affection, like a hug, a kiss, a compliment, or a quick note expressing your appreciation.

- **Active Listening:** Give your partner your undivided attention when they're speaking. Make eye contact, put away distractions, and ask clarifying questions to demonstrate your genuine interest.

- **Share Everyday Moments:** Talk about your day, even the little things. Share your thoughts, feelings, and experiences, creating a sense of connection throughout the day.

CHAPTER 8

- Express Gratitude: Express your gratitude for your partner and the things they do for you. Verbal appreciation goes a long way in strengthening the bond.

- Engage in Shared Activities: Make time for shared activities you both enjoy, even if it's just watching a movie together or taking a walk. This creates positive memories and strengthens your connection.

- Practice Physical Touch: Non-sexual physical touch like holding hands, cuddling, or a gentle massage releases oxytocin, the "love hormone," promoting feelings of closeness and affection.

Weekly Practices:

- Schedule Dedicated "Us Time": Set aside dedicated time each week, even if it's just an hour, to connect deeply with your partner. This could involve having a conversation without distractions, going on a date night, or engaging in a shared activity you both enjoy.

CHAPTER 8

- Practice Empathy Games: Play games or engage in activities that encourage you to see things from your partner's perspective. This can foster deeper understanding and connection.

- Express Appreciation Through Acts of Service: Go above and beyond by doing something nice for your partner that shows you care, like doing a chore they usually do or running an errand for them.

- Reflect and Communicate: Reflect on your connection throughout the week. Discuss what worked well, what challenges you faced, and how you can further strengthen your emotional connection.

Remember:

Consistency is key. Small, intentional actions taken daily and weekly can significantly impact your emotional connection and lead to a more fulfilling and meaningful relationship.

Additional Tips:

- Be present: Put away your phone and other distractions when you're with your partner.

- Be playful and have fun: Laughter and shared enjoyment strengthen emotional connection.

- Be vulnerable: Share your true feelings and experiences to foster deeper intimacy.

- Practice forgiveness: Everyone makes mistakes. Be willing to forgive each other and move forward.

By incorporating these practices into your daily and weekly routine, you can cultivate a strong emotional connection with your partner, enriching your relationship and creating a space for shared growth and happiness.

FROM THE AUTHOR

I hope this handbook has been as enlightening and helpful for you as it has been for me.

Remember, relationships are like gardens – they need nurturing, attention, and a little bit of sunshine to thrive.

So go ahead, water your love with empathy, understanding, and lots of laughter. And don't forget to give yourself and your partner a big ol' hug every now and then!

With Love,

Adele

Made in United States
Cleveland, OH
27 November 2024

11022293R00098